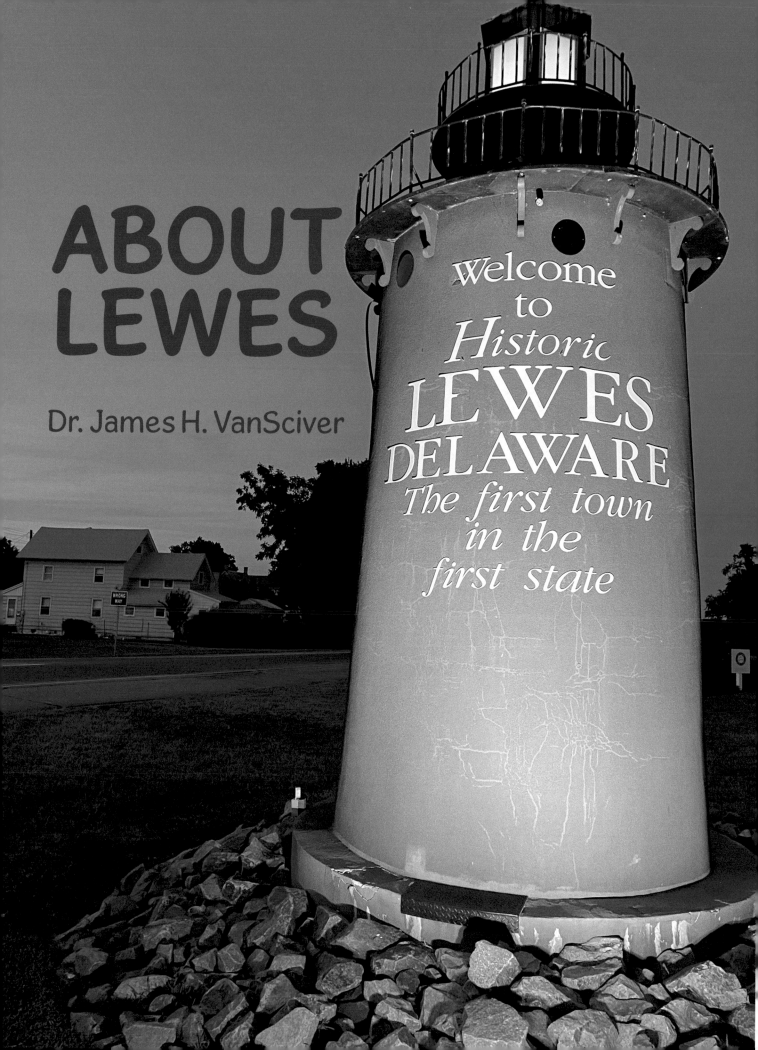

ABOUT LEWES

Dr. James H. VanSciver

welcome to Historic LEWES DELAWARE The first town in the first state

To order additional copies of this book, contact:
Xlibris
844-714-8691
www.Xlibris.com
Orders@Xlibris.com

ISBN: 978-1-6641-9037-5 (sc)
ISBN: 978-1-6641-8962-1 (e)

Print information available on the last page

Rev. date: 08/20/2021

This book is dedicated to all those people whose hard work through history made Lewes the beautiful, charming, clean, and family-friendly fishing village it remains today.

When sailors wanted to stop a ship
Into the water the anchor they'd slip.

A VISIT TO LEWES

I called up a friend who lives far way,
Invited him to Lewes to stay for a day.

The awkward silence I took for a balk,
So, into the phone I started to talk.

Then I said, about this I'll boast.
And told him Lewes was known to the Post.

He listened as I talked about sand
And how he could leave happy and tanned.

I went on talking about places to eat
And explaining to him the meaning of "jeet".

The food is diverse and nice to the taste
The service is great and delivered without haste.

"Jeet" is a colloquialism made of three words,
Did, you, and eat is not said by the nerds.

He took me up and came for a while.
I met him and he said with a smile,

"Your words were true as I soon found.
"Lewes is the happiest place around.

"As I'm walking down the street,
"The nicest people I always meet.

"The homes are well kept, and you know how to broom.
"And I give my compliments to Lewes in Bloom."

When this tower is seen far away,
People know they are close to their stay.

Second Street is truly a visitor's delight
With shopping and food well into the night.

Bookstores, ice cream, and toys cover the place
And a bakery, a flower shop, and bank just in case.

Do you like Indian, Italian, or Hispanic fare?
Or seafood, beef, or anything you care?

No matter your tastes, it's all there.
Just go in a door and pull up a chair.

Gifts, food, and shopping galore
With nothing to equal this on the Shore.

Clothing, shoes, and jewelry aplenty
And toys for little ones there are many.

Pet friendly the town is all year
As leashed dogs with their owners walk very near.

At times no cars are welcome on the street
So, visitors the town's merchants can meet.

I asked my friend his plans and when he would leave.
He said he had other thoughts up his sleeve.

I like Lewes so much more every day.
I think this at this place I would now like to stay.

Walking down Second Street,
You never know who you'll meet.

"Argh!" shouts as this pirate ship nears
Filled with the likes of young buccaneers.

Lewes Unleashed

If you have a dog and he likes to run
There is a place in Lewes where he can have fun.

Lewes Unleashed has gone to the dogs
And people would rather run there than their jogs.

Hounds of all colors, shapes, and sizes.
Each day brings guests more surprises.

The board spends many resources keeping the place green
And, with the help of the visitors, it's also kept clean.

There's a place for the big dogs and another for the small.
And a third area for teaching tricks for the short and the tall.

Canines have water to play in and more just to drink.
The kinds of good times they have is more than you can think.

There's sniffing, running, and games of go fetch
And more running and jumping and some of them catch.

It's no place for growling, biting and the like.
If your dog's into that, you'll be sent for a hike.

It's opened each day from morning to night
The people who go there think that's just right.

There are a couple of rules very visitor must follow.
No treats are allowed, not even bone marrow.

And, if your dog deposits, after it you must run
To keep it from others who may be under the gun.

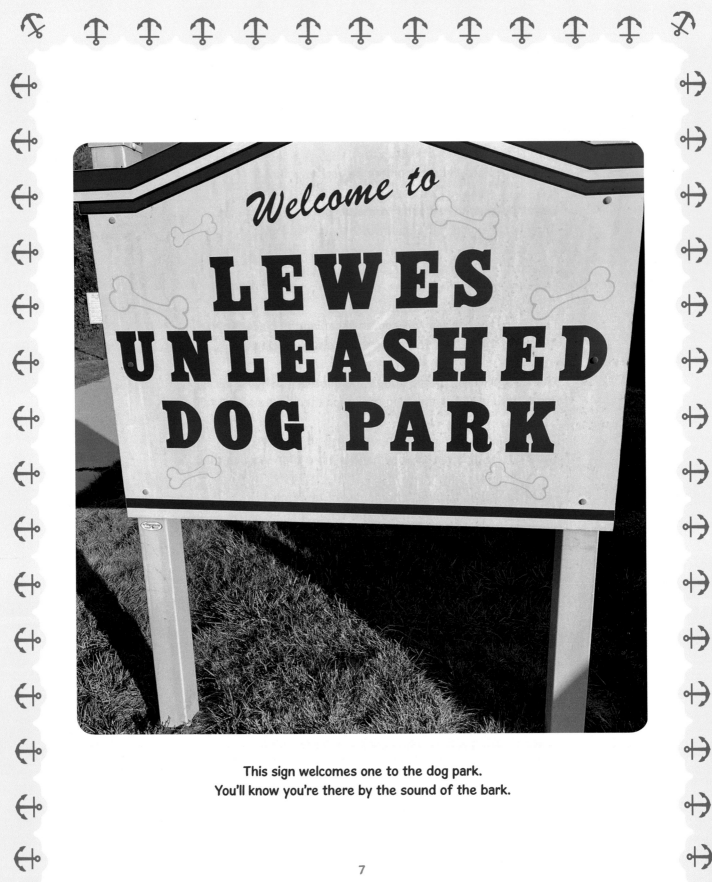

This sign welcomes one to the dog park.
You'll know you're there by the sound of the bark.

In your hand a small bag there must be
To pick up the droppings but not the wet pee.

A repository site is always quite near
With a supply of small bags so owners need not fear.

Three areas fenced in so the dogs can run wild
While their owners' emotions can only be mild.

There are plenty of tennis balls scattered around
So dogs can catch them on the bound.

The training park presents the epitome of synergy
To test and support your dog's energy.

The park rests nearly under the wind mill
And trees surrounding it protect you from chill.

Just turn off New Road and look to the right
Your dog will want to stay there into the night.

The friends he will make he'll miss when you leave
And the next morning he'll be pulling your sleeve.

The humans are not bad as you'll soon discover.
All topics of discussion they daily cover.

So, if you and your pooch would like a good time
Head to Lewes Unleashed and happiness you'll find.

A Lewes Unleashed beautiful dog hat
Given to volunteers, imagine that!

Elvis certainly knows the way.
At the dog park he loves to play.

FORT MILES

If interested in history, you may be
There is a place in Lewes you really must see.

Hidden under sand dunes, the bunkers do tell
The lives of the many who answered the bell.

A fortress so large it drove Lewes' economy
And made short work of the oncoming enemy.

A guardian of the coast against ships and U-boats,
The soldiers took aim as told by their notes.

So good was their firing that nary a craft
Made it past their guns while watching their draft.

A big gun from the Missouri and a piece of the Arizona
Make this place so special in remembering the trauma.

Barracks, powder storage, and lots of guns, too
All polished and waiting just for you.

The guides will inform you as they know their stuff
They'll reveal to you how our army was so tough.

Long hours of hard work it took the volunteers
Much time, sweat, and energy over the years.

The people who built this under the sand
Made a structure so sturdy and totally grand.

God bless the Fort Miles Historical Association
For making this all an exciting visitation.

This tower can for many miles see
Over the land and out to the sea.

THE BEACH

Sand brings a lot of people to town
Just to walk on the shore and then to sit down.

The beach in Lewes is full each summer day
As grownups rest back and children play.

Lifeguards overlook the throngs that show up
Whether in cars, vans, or a rusty pick-up.

Laughter can be heard as the waves tickle the beach
About water safety children's parents do teach.

Better get there early if you want a spot
To enjoy on your blanket when it gets really hot.

The kids will dig for sand fleas and collect shells
While you dream of dinner and delightful food smells.

Musing away the hours with no hassles
While the kids are busy making sandcastles.

Be watchful of the fellas wearing the bright yellow tops
In case in back of your car one looks and then stops.

You don't want to have to reach in your pocket as he asks you to pay.
To do so might ruin the rest of your day.

A day at Lewes Beach is supposed to be fun.
Let nothing deny you your spot in the sun.

The stand of the guard welcomes the sun's rise.
A time for reflection to make yourself wise.

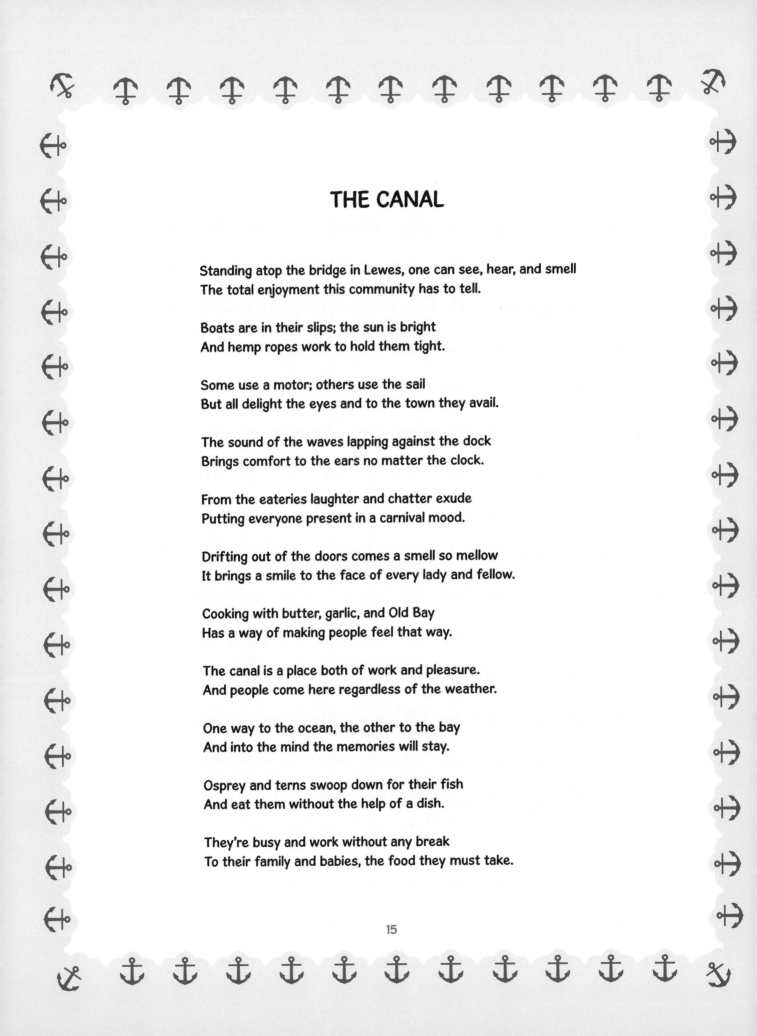

THE CANAL

Standing atop the bridge in Lewes, one can see, hear, and smell
The total enjoyment this community has to tell.

Boats are in their slips; the sun is bright
And hemp ropes work to hold them tight.

Some use a motor; others use the sail
But all delight the eyes and to the town they avail.

The sound of the waves lapping against the dock
Brings comfort to the ears no matter the clock.

From the eateries laughter and chatter exude
Putting everyone present in a carnival mood.

Drifting out of the doors comes a smell so mellow
It brings a smile to the face of every lady and fellow.

Cooking with butter, garlic, and Old Bay
Has a way of making people feel that way.

The canal is a place both of work and pleasure.
And people come here regardless of the weather.

One way to the ocean, the other to the bay
And into the mind the memories will stay.

Osprey and terns swoop down for their fish
And eat them without the help of a dish.

They're busy and work without any break
To their family and babies, the food they must take.

Fishing and eating and fun to be had.
A trip to the canal will soon be your fad.

All this activity can be seen through the fences
The goings on have a way of stimulating the senses.

As darkness descends all over the place
The moon, stars, and lights cover it with grace.

Against the black backdrop it's easy to see
Why so many people at this place come to be.

Reflections from the water double the scene
As the noise from the sides are striking and keen.

And the cacophony of music, people and birds
Provides a sound not defined by words.

The sounds put together brings one word to mind.
Its happiness the term this place does define.

Sounds, scenes, and aroma to mind are all sent
With the delectable sense of a delicious scent.

A gentle breeze to the face, then a sniff
Confirms the joy with only one whiff.

The delights from the bridge all come to pass
When one takes the walk through the grass

And ends up on the deck's planks
For which one will give plenty of thanks.

The canal at night sparkles and glistens
And talks to anyone who stops and listens.

FARMERS MARKET

If you're looking for fresh food to eat
There are some people you just have to meet.

Saturday at George Smith Park they gather
Or Wednesday at the Hammock if you'd rather.

The joy of food for your sight and taste
With nothing left over and nothing to waste.

The Farmers Market is open 'til noon
And, for every person, they will make some room.

The price of asparagus
Will not make you fuss.

And the cost of honey
Will save you some money.

Fruits and vegetables and some baked goods, too.
With some that come from those that moo.

It's local and fresh and fills the place
And given to you by those with grace.

Carrots, berries, and sweet potatoes
With melons, beets, and red tomatoes.

Peas and limas, and squash and broccoli
Everyone leaves mighty happy.

So, if you like lettuce and corn,
Show up at the market in the early morn.

People pack the Farmers' Market grounds.
You can tell by the variety of sounds.

Basket upon basket of delicious peaches
As far as the sight of your eye reaches.

Flowers so pretty as you can tell.
Nice for the sight and great to smell.

So many colors appeal to the eye
With so many choices from which to buy.

A display of lettuce and radish.
A garnish fit for any dish.

No need to go to the bakery shop.
At this place at one table, you just have to stop.

A table loaded with jams and jellies
Which will soon find their way to hungry bellies.

LEWES HISTORICAL SOCIETY

There is a group whose duty it is to oversee
The history of Lewes and all that may be.

The Lewes Historical Society volunteers
Have taken their work seriously over the years.

They point out the Dutch marker from 1631
And of the War of 1812 have some fun.

Lewes was bombarded while the citizens took a swig
And a broken leg troubled a pig.

The only death was a chicken
Who passed before the British took their lickin.

They'll show you the cannon that protected the beach
And tell you about how they prevented a breach.

Their pride and joy is the Cannon House.
Where a ball is still lodged, just missing a mouse.

Then there is quite a fishy story
That describes how Menhaden touched history.

Perhaps their crown jewel is their small community
That looks like it was built five centuries post antiquity.

The Ryves Holt House was built first as an inn
You'll discover why when you first walk in.

Their mission is for Lewes history preservation.
You may join them if you have the inclination.

If on a structure this shield you do see,
You'll know it's part of Lewes history.

This spot marks the first touch of the Dutch.
What they found here didn't amount to that much.

Used to dry the Menhaden fish net.
The men of color worked them when wet.

This house has stood for several centuries
And created for many wonderful memories.

These cannon over Lewes Canal did watch
As the War of 1812 kicked up a notch.

At Lewes the British fired this iron ball
And embedded it deeply into this wall.

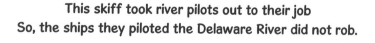

LAST LEWES
PILOT SKIFF
USED TO TAKE DEL. BAY AND RIVER PILOTS
FROM PILOT BOAT PHILADELPHIA AND
PILOT BOAT DELAWARE
TO AND FROM SHIPS IN DEL. BAY
BEFORE WORLD WAR II
ROWED BY 4 APPRENTICE PILOTS
BUILT BY
DAVE WATSON
LEWES
MASTER SMALL BOAT BUILDER
MOTOR LAUNCHES USED AFTER
BEGINNING OF WORLD WAR II

This skiff took river pilots out to their job
So, the ships they piloted the Delaware River did not rob.

It served the U.S. Lighthouse Management well
This old and aging nautical bell.

LEWES IN BLOOM

There's a reason why Lewes looks so beautiful each day.
Lewes in Bloom members work to keep it that way.

Their work is not easy and involves much weeding
That'll work on your hands until they start bleeding.

Their goal is to keep Lewes great looking for everyone
Even if that keeps all their members on the run.

In 2016 for goodness sakes
Lewes was called "The Most Beautiful Small City in the United States!"

So, flowers and shrubs you and others can adore
But the work of these people is much, much more.

They host festivals, trainings, competitions and more.
With wreath-making, children's feats, and even a tour.

Springtime brings tulips a-washing the town
With their bright colors showing all around.

There are flowers for each season of the year
And bright-colored blossoms are always near.

They run their business on donations and dues
So, it's the locals' charity that keeps Lewes in hues.

The next time you walk by a colorful arrangement
Consider the people who made for your contentment.

Lewes in Bloom has been great for the town
Making it the prettiest community around.

These flowers were planted by Lewes in Bloom
Whose goal is every green plot to groom.

PLANTERS TENDED BY
Lewes in Bloom

Lewes in Bloom's volunteers keep watch each day
So their artwork is more than just okay.

The work of volunteers for hours
Produced this beautiful display of flowers.

CAPE MAY LEWES FERRY

The ride is just 17 miles
But the one and one-half hours will be filled with smiles.

A whale or some dolphins you may spot
And osprey, red knots, and egrets or not.

The Cape May Lewes Ferry is open all year
So, missing a trip one does not have to fear.

Pedestrians and cars may both ride.
From the ferry the Lewes rockpile cannot hide.

Three lighthouses the ferry will always pass
Before passengers again set foot on grass.

The Breakwater, Harbor of Refuge, and Cape May will be seen
Their structures standing so tall and lean.

On the second deck is found food and a bar
So, passengers don't have to walk too far.

As the waves against the ferry's hull do lap
It is hard for some riders to not take a nap.

Watch the captain dock the craft
In water deep enough to honor its draft

You'll hear the screeching of ship against piling
As the rubber strains against the ship's sides sliding.

If a peaceful ride on the water comes to mind
On the ferry you have all the joy you can find.

The mouth of the Ferry opens wide
So you can drive your car right inside.

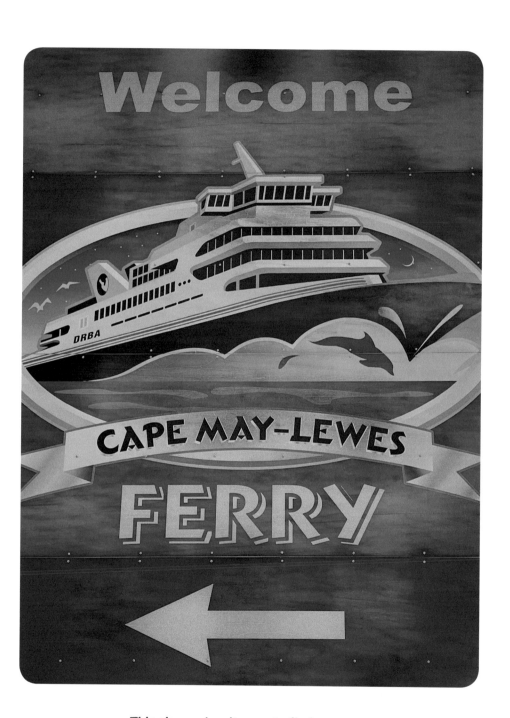

This sign makes it easy to find your way
From the shore of Lewes all the way to Cape May.

ZWAANENDAEL MUSEUM

The iconic Zwaaendael Museum boasts a Dutch architectural flair
While sitting in the middle of Lewes there.

Disclosing maritime, military, and social history
So, the development of the town is no mystery.

David Pieterson DeVries stands upon the roof.
He led the first Dutch settlement and there's proof.

There is no price to enter the door
But the museum survives on donations and more.

You'll see a plate from the wreck of the DeBraack
Look for the chip and then the crack.

And then there's the Manby Mortar
Which shot a line across the water.

Most interesting is the Fiji Merman.
Is it a fish or is it a man?

The museum is filled with fascinating displays
So, you may discover history in many ways.

The artifacts show much of the Dutch
And other ethnic groups and such.

Located in such a beautiful setting
Means more for the experience you will be getting.

Found in this structure are plenty of treasures
A gift to Lewes by all measures.

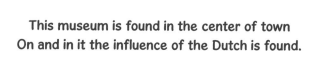

This museum is found in the center of town
On and in it the influence of the Dutch is found.

LIGHTSHIP OVERFALLS

The lightship Overfalls is moored comfortably at the dock
Where people come to visit her nearly round the clock.

An impressive looking older boat
Freshly painted bow to stern.

Her job was keeping others afloat
Work from which she did not turn.

She was a floating lighthouse
And worked day and night.

Her job was to keep the light burning
And burning very bright.

She was the final lighthouse ship built
By the U.S. Lighthouse Service.

So now your hat you should gently tilt
For her role in keeping others from nervous.

She was ordered to stay on station
No matter how severe the weather.

She and her 14-man crew could
Not have done it better.

The Overfalls Foundation seeks to save maritime history
So those who did not shape it will know how it came to be.

The best way to learn about it is to take one of the tours.
It's about time to step on the deck so up with all the oars.

The Lightship Overfalls shines in the night.
Her deck and equipment exposed by the light.

This prop from the Overfalls finally had to stop
And wound up planted right on this spot.

A Town Steeped in History and Filled with Grace

As you are enjoying the sights on your morning walk
About this town Lewes will fill you with talk.

The sights and the sounds are here every day.
And are delightful for your senses in every way.

The canal cuts its way and separates the beach
Yet the bridge makes it possible for you to reach.

Toys for the kids and for the ladies clothes
There's plenty for all as everyone knows.

Souvenirs to point out the town's history
So visitors are not kept in mystery.

There's something for everyone, big and small
And a memory awaits the short and the tall.

Between these covers was spent so much ink
To invite you to look but more so to think.

The town of Lewes is at peace with nature.
The people celebrate and also nurture.

If you are a visitor, we're sure you'll return.
About this place you will forever yearn.

This piece captures some but not all of it
For the rest you'll have to use some of your wit.

As you sigh softly and take your last look
Never forget where you put this grand book.

Printed in the United States
by Baker & Taylor Publisher Services